The Critical Idiom

General Editor: JOHN D. JUMP

6   *Fancy & Imagination*

Fancy & Imagination/*R. L. Brett*

Methuen & Co Ltd

First published 1969
by Methuen & Co Ltd 11 New Fetter Lane London EC4
© 1969 R. L. Brett
Printed in Great Britain
by Cox & Wyman Ltd, Fakenham, Norfolk

SBN 416 15810 2 Hardback
SBN 416 15820 X Paperback

*Distributed in the U.S.A.
by Barnes & Noble Inc.*

PR
4487
.I6
B7

Contents

General Editor's Preface

This volume is one of a series of short studies, each dealing with a single key item, or a group of two or three key items, in our critical vocabulary. The purpose of the series differs from that served by the standard glossaries of literary terms. Many terms are adequately defined for the needs of students by the brief entries in these glossaries, and such terms will not be the subjects of studies in the present series. But there are other terms which cannot be made familiar by means of compact definitions. Students need to grow accustomed to them through simple and straightforward but reasonably full discussions of them. The purpose of this series is to provide such discussions.

Some of the terms in question refer to literary movements (e.g. 'Romanticism', 'Aestheticism', etc.), others to literary kinds (e.g. 'Comedy', 'Epic', etc.), and still others to stylistic features (e.g. 'Irony', 'The Conceit', etc.). Because of this diversity of subject-matter, no attempt has been made to impose a uniform pattern upon the studies. But all authors have tried to provide as full illustrative quotation as possible, to make reference whenever appropriate to more than one literature, and to compose their studies in such a way as to guide readers towards the short bibliographies in which they have made suggestions for further reading.

John D. Jump

University of Manchester

I

Imagination and the Association of Ideas

The terms 'fancy' and 'imagination' are generally associated with the name of Coleridge, especially when they are distinguished from or contrasted with each other. But, of course, they were both used before Coleridge and to understand the precise meanings he attached to them and the distinction he drew between them, it is necessary to look at the history of critical theory. The two terms belong to the various attempts which have been made to explain a work of art by reference to the mental processes involved in artistic creation and, when applied to works of literature, are related to what we call composition. Some critics have held that such accounts of how a work is produced cannot help us to judge its literary merit; or to put their point in more philosophical language, a genetic account has no reference to value. Coleridge believed otherwise, but we must leave this question for later discussion.

It is often said that Aristotle, the first great thinker to concern himself with literary criticism, was not interested in the psychology of composition. There is some truth in this, for Aristotle approached literature from the viewpoint of someone trained in the sciences: with an interest in the object before him rather than in the author. He looked at Greek tragedy as a biologist might look at an organism; something subject to growth and decay, but seen in essence at its maturest, when its growth had fully developed and decay had not yet started. This is why he chose to examine the tragedies of the great classical period of Greek drama and the work of writers such as Sophocles and Euripides. Here, if anywhere, would be found the real nature of tragedy, its structure and its organizing principles. His concern was with tragedy as a species, not with the author's struggle to express himself.

But Aristotle did give some account of the origin of art and as a biologist he described this in scientific terms. Earlier writers such as Homer had associated art with mythology; the poet was inspired by the Muse, who was, significantly, the daughter of memory. This enshrined the belief not only that the imagination was nourished by the images stored in a poet's memory, but also that the poet embodied the tribal memory, that he kept alive in the hearts and minds of his contemporaries the feats of valour, the achievements and tribulations of the past, and transmitted these to future generations. Centuries later, Plato had compared the poetic inspiration to magnetism. As a magnet holds iron rings together by an invisible force, so the Muse binds together the poet and his audience by some mysterious attraction. Poetry, for Plato, was not an art or craft which could be learned; it was a kind of divine ecstasy. 'The poet', he writes in his *Ion*,

> is a light and winged and holy thing, and there is no invention in him until he has been inspired and is out of his senses, and the mind is no longer in him.
>
> (Trans. B. Jowett.)

But the scientific mind of Aristotle was not satisfied with such mythological or metaphorical descriptions of what he thought could be explained in more natural terms. Imitation or representation (*mimesis*) was for man instinctive. As children, we first learn by imitating and we derive pleasure from this process. Here, he maintained in his *Poetics*, is the source of art and the explanation of why we take pleasure in creating and contemplating works of art.

Although Aristotle took a great step forward, he did comparatively little to advance our understanding of the psychology of poetic composition. Indeed, this kind of understanding had to wait until psychology itself began to develop as an independent science. But this was not until the seventeenth century. Throughout the Middle Ages poetic discourse became swallowed up in rhetoric or was seen as an inferior kind of logic; little attention was given to psychological questions concerning its genesis. But if medieval thought on the subject was dominated by Aristotle, Renaissance speculation was based on Plato, or on the attempt to marry Aristotelianism to a Christianized form of Platonism. Shakespeare's famous description of the imagination in *A Midsummer Night's Dream*, which places the poet alongside the lunatic and the lover (and is not love a kind of madness?), is little different from Plato's:

> The lunatic, the lover, and the poet,
> Are of imagination all compact;
> . . . .
> The poet's eye, in a fine frenzy rolling,
> Doth glance from heaven to earth, from earth to heaven;
> And, as imagination bodies forth
> The forms of things unknown, the poet's pen
> Turns them to shapes, and gives to airy nothing
> A local habitation and a name.

(V. i.)

The Elizabethans went further than Plato in their belief that poetry gave one access to truth beyond the scope of reason, for this was a product of a Christian neo-Platonism that saw the imagination as divine, a means of bridging the gulf between Heaven and the world of Nature which had been occasioned by the Fall. Bacon expresses this belief as succinctly as anyone in *The Advancement of Learning*, where he tells us that poetry

> . . . was ever thought to have some participation of divinesse, because it doth raise and erect the Minde, by submitting the shewes of things to the desires of the Mind, whereas reason doth buckle and bowe the Mind unto the Nature of things.

(Bk. II.)

Sir Philip Sidney's *Apologie for Poetrie* contains the fullest and most representative account of Elizabethan literary theory. In the *Apologie* Sidney attempts a synthesis of Aristotle and Plato. Poetry, he declares,

> . . . is an art of imitation, for so Aristotle termeth it in his word *mimesis*, that is to say, a representing, counterfeiting, or figuring forth; to speak metaphorically, a speaking picture, with this end, – to teach and delight.

But he speaks in more neo-Platonic tones when he contrasts the world of art and the world of Nature. Only the poet, he writes,

> . . . lifted up with the vigour of his own invention, doth grow in effect, into another nature, in making things either better than nature bringeth forth, or, quite anew, forms such as never were in nature. . . . Nature never set forth the earth in so rich tapestry as divers poets have done, . . . her world is brazen, the poets only deliver a golden.

It was not until the seventeenth century and the arrival of Thomas Hobbes upon the scene that this amalgam of Greek philosophy and Christian doctrine was disturbed. Hobbes more than any other thinker was the first to give a psychological direction to the development of literary theory. He elaborated a conception of the human mind that was to remain the dominant one in English thought for more than a century. Hobbes was a strict empiricist who believed that all our knowledge derives from sense experience. He declares in the opening chapter of his most famous work, *Leviathan* (1651), that '. . . there is no conception in a man's mind, which hath not at first, totally, or by parts, been begotten upon the organs of sense'. The objects we perceive impinge on our sense organs and produce images in the mind; these images remain stored in the memory when the objects themselves are no longer present, and in one place Hobbes calls the memory simply 'decaying sense' (*Leviathan*, 1, ii). It is from this store of images that the judgement and fancy (or imagination, for Hobbes does not distinguish between them) develop. He elaborates this account of the poetic imagination in a famous passage of his *Answer to D'Avenant* (1650):

> Time and Education begets experience; Experience begets memory; Memory begets Judgement and Fancy; Judgement begets the strength and structure, and Fancy begets the Ornaments of a Poem. The Ancients therefore fabled not absurdly in making memory the Mother of the Muses. For memory is the World (though not really, yet so as in a looking glass) in which the Judgement, the severer Sister, busieth her self in a grave and rigid examination of all the parts of Nature, and in registring by Letters their order, causes, uses, differences, and resemblances; Whereby the Fancy, when any work of Art is to be performed findes her materials at hand and prepared for use.
>
> (*Critical Essays of the Seventeenth Century*, ed. J. E. Spingarn (Oxford, 1908), II, p. 56.)

Fancy, he tells us in *Leviathan*, is the faculty which discerns likenesses whereas the judgement distinguishes differences. Of the two, '. . . fancy, without the help of judgment, is not commended as a virtue: but . . . judgment . . . is commended for itself, without the help of fancy' (I, viii). Indeed, he writes,

> . . . without steadiness, and direction to some end, a great fancy is one kind of madness; such as they have, that entering into any discourse, are snatched from their purpose, by every thing that comes in their thoughts.
>
> (I, viii.)

One can see that, for Hobbes, the fancy or imagination needs to be held in strict check by the judgement. It is a faculty which helps a writer put his thought in fresh and persuasive terms, but is not in itself a rational activity. When it is controlled and guided by the judgement it is a very powerful instrument in moving the hearts and minds of men.

But so far forth as the Fancy of man has traced the ways of true Philosophy, so far it hath produced very marvellous effects to the benefit of mankinde. All that is beautiful or defensible in building, or marvellous in Engines and Instruments of motion, whatsoever commodity men receive from the observations of the Heavens, from the description of the Earth, from the account of Time, from walking on the Sea, and whatsoever distinguisheth the civility of Europe from the Barbarity of the American savages, is the Workmanship of Fancy but guided by the Precepts of true Philosophy.

Furthermore, when the moral philosopher fails to induce men to lead virtuous lives because his teaching is too abstract and his precepts too austere, the poet may find a more willing audience because he provides concrete examples of the beauty of holiness. For, Hobbes continues,

> . . . where these precepts fail, as they have hitherto failed in the doctrine [i.e. teaching] of Moral vertue, there the Architect, Fancy, must take the Philosophers part upon her self.
>
> (*The Answer to D'Avenant*, ed. cit., II, pp. 59–60.)

It is clear that Hobbes sees the imagination as serving a rhetorical and not a logical purpose; its function is to clothe thought in attractive language, but it has no place in strictly logical discourse itself.

> In demonstration, in counsel, and all rigorous search of truth, judgement does all, except sometimes the understanding have need to be opened by some apt similitude; and then there is so much use of fancy. But for metaphors, they are in this case utterly excluded. For seeing they openly profess deceit; to admit them into counsel, or reasoning, were manifest folly.
>
> (*Leviathan*, I, viii.)

This account by Hobbes of the role of the imagination combines orthodox Renaissance theory with a new psychological approach. He follows the Renaissance writers in regarding the imagination as the servant of the philosopher and the moralist; its function being to provide an attractive dress for the wisdom and virtue they wish to expound. In this Hobbes is a traditionalist. But he breaks new ground in the psychological description he gives of the mental processes involved in composition. The imagination need no longer be a kind of madness or ecstasy, though in dreams and uncontrolled fantasies it amounts to this. It is fundamentally a form of memory, but a memory freed to some degree from the restrictions of actual experience. It can ransack the storehouse of sense images laid up in the memory and, when controlled by an artistic purpose, can associate them in new and pleasing patterns. It cannot, of course, invent something entirely new for its material all comes from sense experience, but it can transcend the limitations of historical fact. Like Aristotle, Hobbes regards the poet as superior to the historian, but not superior to the philosopher.

Dryden, who was a disciple of Hobbes in political theory, adopted also his account of poetic composition and gave it a wide currency. Hobbes, as we have seen, more or less identified memory and imagination. 'Imagination and memory', he writes in *Leviathan*, 'are but one thing, which for divers considerations hath divers names' (I, ii). The act of composition involves turning over the images stored in the memory, as one might turn over the cards in a filing system; or, in Hobbes's own words, 'as one would sweep a room, to find a jewel; or as a spaniel ranges the field till he find a scent; or as a man should run over the alphabet, to start a rhyme' (*Op. cit.*, I, iii). Dryden in the preface to *Annus Mirabilis* uses the same figure of the dog when he writes:

> The faculty of imagination in the writer . . . like a nimble spaniel, beats over and ranges through the field of memory, till it springs the quarry it hunted after.
>
> (*Essays*, ed. W. P. Ker (Oxford, 1900), I, p. 14.)

Indeed, it is obvious that Dryden's account of poetic composition is fundamentally the same as Hobbes's, for he continues:

So then the first happiness of the poet's imagination is properly invention, or finding of the thought; the second is fancy, or the variation deriving, or moulding, of that thought, as the judgment represents it proper to the subject; the third is elocution, or the art of clothing and adorning that thought, so found and varied, in apt, significant, and sounding words: the quickness of the imagination is seen in the invention, the fertility in the fancy, and the accuracy in the expression.

(*Ibid.*, p. 15.)

Hobbes's description of the mind did not pass unchallenged, but before we come to deal with those who criticized it, we must first look at those who developed and extended this description. For these included the most influential thinkers of the eighteenth century, who laid the foundations of what was to become the generally accepted aesthetic theory of the period. Chief of these was John Locke, whose 'new way of ideas' provided a framework which explained the workings of the human mind. Locke, like Hobbes, was an empiricist; that is, he believed all our knowledge (apart from the existence of God, which he believed could be demonstrated, and our knowledge of other selves which was a matter of direct intuition) is derived from experience. In his *Essay Concerning Human Understanding* (1690) he compared the human mind to a blank sheet of paper on which the outside world makes impressions; in the initial stage of perception the mind is passive and knowledge is arrived at by relating the ideas left in the mind by sensation. He follows Hobbes in recognizing two powers of the mind, one which sees resemblances between ideas and the other which distinguishes differences between them. What he describes as 'wit' in the following passage of his *Essay* is very much what Hobbes meant by 'imagination'.

For wit lying most in the assemblage of ideas, and putting those together with quickness and variety, wherein can be found any resemblance or congruity, thereby to make up pleasant pictures and agreeable visions in the fancy; judgment, on the contrary, lies quite on the other side, in separating carefully, one from another, ideas wherein can be found the least difference, thereby to avoid being misled by similitude.

(II, xi.)

But his attitude towards imaginative writing is more austere and grudging than Hobbes's, for where Hobbes was a man with a life-long interest in literature who numbered many poets among his friends, Locke viewed the arts with a certain suspicion.

Since wit and fancy find easier entertainment in the world than dry truth and real knowledge, figurative speeches and allusion in language will hardly be admitted as an imperfection or abuse of it. I confess, in discourses where we seek rather pleasure and delight than information and improvement, such ornaments as are borrowed from them can scarce pass for faults. But yet . . . we must allow that all the art of rhetoric . . . all the artificial and figurative application of words eloquence hath invented, are for nothing else but to insinuate wrong ideas, move the passions, and thereby mislead the judgment.

(III, x.)

Furthermore, Locke developed a theory concerning the 'association of ideas' which again gave a hostile slant to what Hobbes had written about the imagination. The term itself was coined by Locke when he added a chapter on the subject to the fourth edition of his *Essay* in 1700, but the phenomenon of how one idea may call up another in consciousness had been recognized as long ago as Aristotle. It was Hobbes, however, who linked it to the imaginative process. The power of the fancy to relate similar images is augmented, as he realized, by the mental habit we all have of contiguous association, that is the ability of one image to recall another that has previously been connected with it. Thus the scent of lavender which we are now experiencing will recall an image of the cottage where we spent our holidays, because lavender grew in the garden there. This free kind of association, as Hobbes well knew, could be more a feature of dreams than art; in his opinion it needed the control of the judgement and this is why he attached importance to causality as another factor in association. For the memory often associates an event with its cause or with its effect and this will achieve the probability that is desirable in a work of literature. Here again fancy is disciplined by judgement, for the perception of causality is a matter of logic and not rhetoric.

Locke regarded the power of the mind to associate ideas as generally dangerous. Ideas may be associated naturally, that is, corresponding to the order of experience, or logically, but all too often men make irrational connexions between ideas and through repeated and false associations come to build up habits of error and prejudice in their thinking. Locke himself did not attempt to relate his theory of the association of ideas directly to the imagination, but his treatment of the subject obviously suggests a diminished status for poetry. More important than this, however, was the enormous influence of Locke's *Essay* which popularized the association of ideas as a psychological theory and led to further developments in aesthetics and literary criticism. The first critic to apply Locke's theory to criticism was Addison, whose *Spectator* papers on *The Pleasures of the Imagination* had a far wider circulation than even Locke's *Essay*. Addison transformed the theory from a matter of interest only to professional philosophers into a vogue that affected the general sensibility of his age. More than this, his treatment of it led poets and their readers to look in poetry not only for clear and exact ideas, but for the emotional associations that imagery aroused. The influence of both French literature and the Royal Society had conspired to bring poetry close to prose, to persuade men to value what Thomas Sprat, in his *History of the Royal Society* (1667), had described as 'a close, naked, natural way of speaking'. But now Addison's essays encouraged readers to set as much store on the connotations of words as on what they denoted. There is hardly any limit to where the imagination can lead the mind of the reader through its associative power, for, writes Addison,

> . . . any single Circumstance of what we have formerly seen often raises up a whole Scene of Imagery, and awakens numberless Ideas that before slept in the Imagination; such a particular Smell or Colour is able to fill the Mind, on a sudden, with the Picture of the Fields or Gardens, where we first met with it, and to bring up into View all the Variety of Images that once attended it. Our imagination takes the Hint, and leads us unexpectedly into Cities or Theatres, Plains or Meadows.

(*Spectator*, No. 417.)

Although Addison's view of the imagination tied it to the memory, his influence on literary criticism was a liberalizing one. But before we deal with this influence we must sketch the development of the associationist psychology by two other eighteenth-century thinkers, David Hartley and David Hume. Hartley was a disciple of Locke and, like his master, he emphasized the importance of sensation as the source of knowledge, including our moral principles. Morality, according to Hartley, was the product of experience and he repudiated the views of those philosophers who argued that moral ideas are innate. Morality for Hartley is based upon the association of ideas and especially the association of evil with pain, and good with pleasure. This kind of psychological hedonism argued that we are led to a life of virtue because doing good affords us pleasure, and that a refined form of self-satisfaction is the mainspring of morality. What gave Hartley novelty as a writer was his restatement of the associationist theory in physiological terms. His *Observations on Man* first appeared in 1749, and his views were given a wider circulation in a condensed version of this work produced by Joseph Priestley with the title, *Hartley's Theory of the Human Mind*. Hartley's account of the mind described the material of consciousness as firstly, sensations; secondly,

B

simple ideas or images which are copies of sensations, or sensations which remain after the sense objects which cause them have been removed; and thirdly, complex ideas which are produced by relating simple ideas together. These correspond to the three stages of sensation, memory and thought. The principle by which the mind operates is the association of ideas according to contiguity in time and space, and the frequency with which ideas have been related in the past. Hartley then attempts an explanation of our mental processes in terms of physiology or neurology. Outside objects impinge upon the sense organs and set up vibrations in the nervous system and brain. Even when the objects are no longer present, these vibrations will continue, though with diminishing force, and can be re-activated by the association of ideas. In certain respects Hartley's account is not unlike modern theories which take as a model of the mind the computer with its memory stored in electrical circuits which function when triggered by the appropriate signal.

Hume had less popular appeal, perhaps, than Hartley, but he was a more radical thinker who carried empiricism to an extreme conclusion and in doing so provoked the opposition of Kant, who said it was Hume's scepticism which aroused him from his 'dogmatic slumbers'. Hume's *Treatise of Human Nature* appeared in 1739 and his *Enquiry Concerning Human Understanding* in 1748. Although Locke had seen knowledge in terms of reason operating upon the materials of sense experience, he had believed that the objects of sense experience belonged to an external world governed by the law of causality. For Hume, however, causality is reduced to association:

> When the mind, therefore, passes from the idea or impression of one object to the idea or belief of another, it is not determined by reason, but by certain principles, which associate together the ideas of these objects and unite them in the imagination.
>
> (*Treatise*, Bk. I, Part iii, vi.)

The imagination is little more than a name for this associative process by which ideas are related according to their resemblance, their contiguity and the frequency of their previous association. The repetition of the same ideas in the same order of succession leads men to think these ideas to be causally connected, but Hume argues that there is no logical necessity in such connexions; they are merely a matter of custom. His scepticism leads him to deny the continued existence of objects distinct from the perceiving mind and, further, to deny the continued existence of a perceiving self. We have no permanent idea of a continuing self, but merely a succession of discrete and ever-changing impressions. We are, in fact, 'nothing but a bundle or collection of different perceptions'. Though Hume omitted this extreme argument from the *Enquiry*, his philosophical position is one of great scepticism concerning human knowledge and one that leaves the imagination as no more than a form of memory, of which he says, 'the difference betwixt it and the imagination lies in its superior force and vivacity' (*Treatise*, Bk. I, Part iii, v).

We have seen already, that by extending the principle of association to emotions as well as ideas, Addison laid a foundation which accounted for differences of taste. 'It may be here worth our while,' he writes,

> to examine, how it comes to pass that several Readers, who are all acquainted with the same Language, and know the Meaning of the Words they read, should nevertheless have a different Relish of the same Descriptions. We find one transported with a Passage, which another runs over with Coldness and Indifference.

The explanation, of course, is that the passage arouses different associations in various readers.

> This different Taste must proceed either from the Perfection of Imagination in one more than in another, or from the different Ideas that several Readers affix to the same Words.

(*Spectator*, No. 416.)

Addison is not content to leave taste as a matter of individual preference but is anxious to establish a standard which is universal. In this he is grappling with a problem which exercised a long succession of writers in the eighteenth century, but the point of importance for our present discussion is his emphasis upon the part played by the feelings in our response to imagery and upon the part played by taste in our aesthetic judgements. In both respects he is a writer who stands at the beginning of a movement towards Romanticism. Important as this is, however, Addison's treatment of the imagination is limited by his concern with poetic appreciation rather than poetic composition and by his acceptance of association as the main psychological principle. For any radical opposition to the view of the imagination we have been sketching we have to look to writers who belonged to a philosophical tradition different from that of Hobbes and Locke.

Even after Hobbes had written his *Leviathan*, Milton could open *Paradise Lost* with an invocation to God, just as Homer invokes the heavenly Muse at the beginning of his two great epics. Nor was this a mere literary flourish on Milton's part; indeed at the beginning of Book IX of his poem he writes of

> My celestial Patroness, who deigns
> Her nightly visitation unimplor'd,
> And dictates to me slumb'ring, or inspires
> Easy my unpremeditated verse,

and as a devout Christian he believed that his work was inspired by God's spirit. In his *Reason of Church Government* (1642) he had already written of the help vouchsafed to him not 'by the invocation of Dame Memory and her Siren daughters, but by devout prayer to that eternal Spirit who can enrich with all utterance and knowledge'. In his *Answer to D'Avenant*, Hobbes dismisses contemptuously any such notion, especially when made by a Christian poet. 'But why,' he writes, a Christian should think it an ornament to his Poem, either to profane the true God or invoke a false one, I can imagin no cause but a reasonless imitation of Custom, of a foolish custome, by which a man, enabled to speak wisely from the principles of nature and his own meditation, loves rather to speak by inspiration, like a Bagpipe.

(*Critical Essays of the Seventeenth Century*, II, p. 130.)

His sceptical common-sense and psychological acumen combine with his most caustic style to sweep away the idea that God might speak to men directly, either awake or in dreams. 'For,' he declares in his *Leviathan*,

if a man pretend to me, that God hath spoken to him supernaturally and immediately, and I make doubt of it, I cannot easily perceive what argument he can produce, to oblige me to believe it. . . . To say he hath spoken to him in a dream, is no more than to say he dreamed that God spake to him. (III, xxxii.)

Milton was a Christian Platonist and it was a group of men with similar beliefs, the Cambridge Platonists, who first countered Hobbes's philosophy. A contemporary, Gilbert Burnet, Bishop of Salisbury, describes this Cambridge group and their struggle to refute Hobbes's doctrines:

Hobbes, who had long followed the Court, and passed there for a mathematical man, tho' he really knew little that way, . . . came into England in Cromwell's time, and published a very wicked work, with a very strange title, *The Leviathan* . . . He seemed to think that the universe was God, and that souls were material, Thought being only subtil and unperceptible motion. He thought interest and fear were the chief principles of society: And he put all morality in the following that which was our own private will or advantage . . . So this set of men at Cambridge studied to assert, and examine the principles of religion and morality on clear grounds, and in a philosophical method. (Burnet's *History of his Own Time*, pubd. posthumously, 1724–34, Vol. I, p. 186.)

The Cambridge Platonists fought against Hobbes's views along a wide front whose sectors comprised theology, metaphysics, ethics, and theory of knowledge. But fundamentally they all disagreed with his reduction of reality to matter and motion. For, as Ralph Cudworth, one of the leading Platonists, who was Master of Milton's college at Cambridge, wrote in his *True Intellectual System* (1678), the followers of Hobbes allowed

> . . . no other causes of things as philosophical, save the material and mechanical only; this being really to banish all mental, and consequently divine causality, quite out of the world; and to make the whole world to be nothing else but a mere heap of dust, fortuitously agitated.

(I, p. 217.)

The Hobbists, as they were called, had turned God into 'an idle spectator of the various results of the fortuitous and necessary motions of bodies'. There seemed hardly any place left for the spiritual, and certainly none for the miraculous, for everything worked inexorably according to the laws of matter in motion. Cudworth continues:

> They made a kind of dead and wooden world, as it were a carved statue, that hath nothing neither vital nor magical at all in it.

(p. 221.)

In particular Cudworth repudiated Hobbes's account of how we perceive and come to have knowledge. Against Hobbes's empiricism he elaborated an idealist philosophy which saw the mind as creative and active in perception rather than as the passive receptacle of sense impressions from the external world. To illustrate this he takes as an example our perception of a white triangle. On Hobbes's theory our perception is simply the association of sense data such as the whiteness, the triangular shape, and any other sense qualities which constitute the appearance of the triangle. Cudworth declares that such an account omits the power of the mind to perceive objects as objects. Qualities such as whiteness and triangularity are not just particular sense data; they are concepts and we recognize them as qualities which belong to other objects as well as the particular triangle we are perceiving at the moment. For Hobbes 'whiteness' is merely a name, it has no real existence; what is real are particulars. Cudworth, on the other hand, was a Platonist, who believed that such general ideas are real and apprehended by the reason; the knowledge given us by the senses is only of appearances. Reason in man is not a product of sense experience but is innate.

The Cambridge Platonists were not especially interested in aesthetics, though some of their number like John Norris and Henry More were poets as well as philosophers. But their philosophy challenged Hobbes's account of the mind and therefore of the imagination. The first English philosopher to concern himself with aesthetics in any serious way was the third Earl of Shaftesbury, who, though Locke had been his tutor, regarded himself as a disciple of the Cambridge circle. Much as Shaftesbury admired his old tutor, he considered his empiricism to be in the Hobbesian tradition. Indeed, he felt Locke's influence to be even more dangerous, for while Hobbes's religious and political opinion had made him an object of suspicion and even hate, Locke was a respected figure. Writing to a young protégé, who was an undergraduate at Oxford, he expresses it thus:

> Mr. Locke, as much as I honour him on account of other writings ... and as well as I knew him, and can answer for his sincerity as a most zealous *Christian* and believer, did however go in the self-same track [as Hobbes]. . . . 'Twas Mr. Locke, that struck the home blow: for Mr. Hobbes's character and base slavish principles in government took off the poyson of his philosophy.
>
> (*Letters to a Young Man at the University*, 1716.)

Locke, in his *Essay Concerning Human Understanding*, had attacked the notion that the mind possesses innate ideas, but Shaftesbury maintains that Locke was knocking down a figure of straw. The question is not whether we are born with certain ideas already in the mind, but whether we are obliged in the course of interpreting experience to frame ideas which do not themselves derive from experience. '*Innate*,' he continues,

> is a word he poorly plays upon: the right word, tho' less used, is *connatural*, for what has *birth* or *progress* of the *foetus* out of the womb to do in this case? the question is not about the *time* the ideas enter'd, or the moment that one body came out of the other: but whether the constitution of man be such, that sooner or later (no matter when) the idea and sense of *order, administration*, and a God will not infallibly, inevitably, necessarily spring up in him.
>
> (*Ibid.*)

Shaftesbury rejects Locke's comparison of the mind with a blank sheet of paper and the belief that knowledge derives only from sense experience. He holds that the mind is creative and that this power comes from God who created man in his own image.

> . . . the mind conceiving of itself, can only be . . . assisted in the birth. Its pregnancy is from its own nature. Nor could it ever have been thus impregnated by any other mind than that which formed it at the beginning; and which . . . is original to all mental as well as other beauty.
>
> (*Characteristics*, II, p. 135.)

Hobbes's associationist psychology was closely related to his picture of reality as matter in motion. For Shaftesbury the human mind reflects a world of nature which is organic. His Platonism led him to believe that beyond the natural order there is a transcendent and ideal world to which this present world only approximates. But the ideal reveals itself not in the fixed and dead entities of a mechanical construction; it is embodied in the changing forms of a world which is a living and organic growth. Art which is an imitation or representation of nature must then also be creation in a real sense, and poetic invention must be a creative process. In the notes which he left for his unpublished work *Second Characters*, Shaftesbury extends his disagreement with Hobbes and Locke to embrace aesthetics:

> Hence Hobbes, Locke, etc., still the same man, same genus at the bottom. – 'Beauty is nothing'. – 'Virtue is nothing'. – So 'perspective nothing'. – Music nothing'. – but these are the greatest realities of things, especially the beauty and order of affections. These philosophers together with the anti-virtuosi may be called by one common name, viz. barbar[ians].
>
> (*Second Characters*, p. 178.)

In place of an associationist psychology Shaftesbury gives us a picture of the mind made in the image of the divine mind, one which is genuinely creative. The indifferent artist may produce work by bringing together from memory the bits and pieces of his material, by what Shaftesbury calls 'an injudicious random use of wit and fancy'.

> But for the man who truly and in a just sense deserves the name of poet, and who as a real master, or architect in the kind, can describe both men and manners, and give to an action its just body and proportions, he will be found, if I mistake not, a very different creature. Such a poet is indeed a second *Maker*; a just Prometheus under Jove. Like that sovereign artist or universal plastic nature, he forms a whole, coherent and proportioned in itself, with due subjection and subordinacy of constituent parts.
>
> (*Characteristics*, I, 135–6.)

Shaftesbury takes the term 'plastic nature' from Cudworth, who used it to refer to a principle which he believed to be at work in the natural world. This principle is an agent of the divine mind, which animates the whole of creation; for the world was not brought about in one determinate act but is constantly sustained by the divine presence. The poet, like God, creates his world not by assembling mechanically the raw material on which he works, not by stamping this material as wax is stamped by a seal, but by an organic process corresponding more to gestation. The active principle in the poet's mind which is analogous to the 'plastic nature', is the shaping spirit of imagination, which embodies the poet's thought in sensible forms, just as the creation is the embodiment of God's thought.

Although Shaftesbury repudiated the association of ideas as an explanation of the imagination, he never substituted for it an adequate psychology of poetic composition, nor did he really come to terms with Locke on his own ground of epistemology. But one should not underestimate Shaftesbury's importance. In two respects especially he heralded a Romantic conception of poetry and of the poetic imagination. The first of these was the analogy he drew between the mind of God and the mind of the poet; the second was his conviction that Nature is not a machine but an organism. Both of these, as we shall see, are important for an understanding of Coleridge. There is an historical irony in the fact that Coleridge, voracious reader though he was, seems to have been unaware of Shaftesbury's writings, whereas in Germany Shaftesbury was an influential figure and known to a succession of writers such as Lessing, Herder, Kant and Schiller, all of whom came to be regarded in England as prophets of a new movement. At home his importance was diminished throughout the century by the prevalence of an empiricist philosophy, and even his own followers were so impressed with the authority of Locke that they tried to accommodate his views to the 'new way of ideas'.

Akenside's long poem *The Pleasures of the Imagination* (1744) is obviously indebted to the *Spectator* papers of the same name, but it contains a Platonic strain which owes something to Shaftesbury, and Akenside acknowledges this in the notes and the text of his poem. Like Addison, Akenside places the imagination between the senses and the understanding; indeed the point is made at the very beginning of the *Design* to his poem where he writes:

> There are certain powers in human nature which seem to hold a middle place between the organs of sense and the faculties of moral perception: they have been called by a very general name, The Powers of Imagination.

This echoes *Spectator* 411 in which Addison describes 'the pleasures of the imagination' as 'not so gross as those of sense, nor so refined as those of the understanding'. In other words, both of them see works of art as less concrete than sense objects but less abstract than concepts. In this they anticipate Coleridge, who regarded the imagination as a mediating faculty between sense perception and the understanding. If either had developed this insight it could have led to a theory of the imagination as a source of symbols which combine the qualities of particularity and generalization, but as it was, they were too much dominated by Locke and more concerned with the part played by the imagination in the appreciation of poetry than with poetic invention. Akenside indicates in one of his Odes the compromise he sought to achieve between Platonism and what he considers to be a modern account of the mind, though here it is Bacon he mentions and not Locke.

> Beauty with Truth I strive to join,
> And grave assent with glad applause;
> To paint the story of the soul,
> And Plato's visions to control
> By Verulamian laws.   *(Ode* xvi.)

Few writers, however Romantic in other respects they might be, achieved more than this kind of compromise when they explored the poetic imagination. Although Burke extended the notion of aesthetic appreciation to include the sublime as well as the beautiful, he could write only in the following terms about the imagination:

> The mind of man possesses a sort of creative power of its own; either in representing at pleasure the images of things in the order and

manner in which they were received by the senses, or in combining those images in a new manner, and according to a different order. This power is called imagination; and to this belongs whatever is called wit, fancy, invention and the like.

(*On Taste.*)

Although Burke calls the imagination creative it is really no more than a reproductive or associative faculty in the analysis he gives us. Alexander Gerard in his *Essay on Genius* (1774) advances little further when he tells us that genius is connected with 'a peculiar vigour of association'. All men have this power of association, he argues, but the man of genius possesses it in abundance. Even so, his analysis is forced back upon the vague use of 'magic' when he tries to explain genius, for the man of genius is one whose fertility of association will cause ideas to 'rush into his view as if they were conjured up by the force of magic'.

There was, however, one great poet at the end of the century whose understanding of his own genius led him to an altogether more radical appraisal of the imagination. This was William Blake, who throughout his life waged war against the empiricist tradition, or what he called the 'philosophy of the five senses'. In his *Everlasting Gospel* he wrote:

> This life's five windows of the soul
> Distorts the Heavens from pole to pole,
> And leads you to believe a lie
> When you see with, not through, the eye.

Here he is saying in verse what he had said much earlier in his two little tracts *There is no Natural Religion* and *All Religions are One*. In the first of these prose works he challenges Locke's doctrine that 'Man cannot naturally Perceive but through his natural or bodily organs', and argues that 'Man's perceptions are not bounded by organs of perception; he perceives more than sense (tho' ever so acute) can discover . . . The desire of Man being Infinite, the possession is Infinite and himself Infinite. He who sees the Infinite in all things, sees God'. Blake insists on the power of the mind to go beyond sense experience in framing those ideas and values which are part of man's spiritual endowment. In the second of his tracts Blake describes the poet as one especially gifted in this way.

Alongside Locke, Blake placed Newton as his other great enemy. These two had shaped the intellectual life of the eighteenth century and, in Blake's view, had shaped it disastrously. Locke had built an intellectual structure for the internal life of the mind, and Newton had built a similar structure for the external world of nature. Newton had explained the Universe in terms of mathematics and had given greater precision to Hobbes's account of reality as matter in motion. The Universe was a great machine, devoid of any colour, scent or sound. These secondary qualities, as Locke was able to explain, were simply subjective modes of apprehending matter in motion. Locke's picture of the mind as a blank sheet of paper affronted Blake's most deeply held convictions, for the poet believed that the human soul exists before birth and brings with it into life an intuitive wisdom from the transcendent world it has left behind. For him the world of nature is a reflection and revelation of this other world; an outward and visible symbol of the spiritual meaning that lies behind appearances. Newton and Locke had turned the Universe into a Universe of death; Blake saw it as a living Universe in which everything has a spiritual significance. The ability to recognize these significances and embody them in poetic visions was for Blake the faculty of imagination.

Blake's convictions were confirmed and extended by a wide but eclectic reading in the works of the neo-Platonists, Cabbalists and Swedenborgians and this eclecticism has made it more difficult, even to the present day, for his readers to understand him. T. S. Eliot was referring to the unsystematic and unacademic character of Blake's thought when he wrote: 'We have the same respect for Blake's philosophy . . . that we have for an ingenious piece of home-made furniture: we admire the man who has put it together out of the odds and ends about the house' (T. S. Eliot, *Selected Prose*, ed. John Hayward, 1953, p. 171). The stricture is a very strong one, but there is a good deal of truth in it, for Blake was a mystic and a visionary rather than a philosopher. Something of the same kind could be said even of his poetic idiom. The profundity of his poetry has often been obscured because of his occult language and the deeply personal nature of his vision. Though Blake's own poetic vision was profound and though his understanding of the imagination was a penetrating one, it required someone with greater powers of philosophical analysis to challenge in intellectual terms the basic assumptions of eighteenth-century thought. For this we must turn to Coleridge.

2

Coleridge's Distinction between Fancy and Imagination

Coleridge's theory of the imagination is given its fullest exposition in his *Biographia Literaria*, which was written in 1815 and published in 1817. The sub-title of this work, *Biographical Sketches of My Literary Life and Opinions*, is an indication that the book is not a straightforward theoretical exposition. In fact, a good deal of the work is an account of Coleridge's intellectual development, of the doctrines he had once held and then discarded, as well as those he is now convinced are true. Many readers are bewildered by it and find its argument difficult to follow; a good many skip some of the chapters because they find them obscure or irrelevant. One can agree that as a straightforward account of Coleridge's literary theory it is not entirely satisfactory, for in places it is unnecessarily prolix and in others it is tantalizingly brief. In particular, he does not provide the sustained discussion of the nature of the poetic imagination we would have liked.

But two criticisms of the work which are often made are in fact misplaced. The first is advanced by those who object to the mixing of autobiography and philosophy. Such an objection would have gained little sympathy from Coleridge, who believed that ideas are not remote and detached from the personality of the man who holds them. Coleridge held that ideas energize a man's mind and work their way into his personality so that they affect his conduct; a man's life and a man's opinions are, in the end, inseparable. The search for the right ideas is a search for something which will satisfy a man's deepest needs and therefore there can be no divorce between life and the intellect.

The other objection is made by those who dislike Coleridge's mixing of poetics and philosophy. For them poetry and even literary criticism have little connexion with philosophy and they regard Coleridge as a poet *manqué*, or as a poet who after a few splendid years of creative achievement lost his way in the thickets of metaphysical speculation. They see Coleridge's interest in philosophy as a dangerous preoccupation which stifled his poetic genius, or they feel, in the words of his own ode, *Dejection*, that abstruse research had stolen from his nature all the natural man. Some writers, who regard literary criticism as a matter of sensibility rather than abstract thought, have gone even further and produced a tripartite Coleridge in which the philosopher, the poet and the critic were all frustrating each other. But this flies in the face of both the facts of Coleridge's life and what he himself said. Coleridge was always interested in philosophy, even at the period when he was writing his greatest poetry, and there is no reason to believe that any decline in his poetic powers was brought about by this interest. Moreover, he himself thought that poetry and philosophy were kindred activities. 'No man', he observes in Chapter XV of *Biographia Literaria*, 'was ever yet a great poet without being at the same time a profound philosopher.'[1] Coleridge constantly sought for unity of the personality and believed that the poetic imagination was a means of achieving this. 'The poet,' he writes,

> described in *ideal* perfection, brings the whole soul of man into activity, with the subordination of its faculties to each other, according to their relative worth and dignity. He diffuses a tone and spirit of unity, that blends, and (as it were) *fuses*, each into each, by that synthetic [i.e. synthesizing] and magical power, to which we have exclusively appropriated the name of imagination.   (II, p. 12.)

[1] *Op. cit.*, ed. Shawcross, Oxford, 1907, II, p. 19. All references are to this edition.

We shall be concerned, then, with Coleridge's account of the imagination as a philosophical theory, but we shall relate this to literary criticism and to the nature of poetry itself, realizing that for him they were all part of a single enterprise. Indeed, when he embarked upon *Biographia Literaria* Coleridge's design was to write a preface for an edition of his poems, setting out what he considered to be the principles of criticism in art generally and poetry in particular. This design was abandoned as he wrote, and the lengthy essay he elaborated in its place became the intellectual history of his opinions, and especially the part played by art and the imagination in his general philosophy. Nevertheless, we can discern something of this design. The first part of his work is devoted to the development of his philosophy and this culminates in his account of the imagination. The second part turns to a lengthy critical analysis of the poetry and critical theories of his friend Wordsworth. There is no real inconsistency here; for Wordsworth was at once the source and touchstone of what he believed to be the nature of the poetic imagination.

Coleridge tells us that it was in his twenty-fourth year, that is, in 1795/6, when he heard Wordsworth reading his own poetry, that he was first led to speculate about the imagination and that 're-peated meditations' on the subject led him later to

suspect . . . that Fancy and Imagination were two distinct and widely different faculties, instead of being, according to the general belief, either two names with one meaning, or, at furthest, the lower and higher degree of one and the same power.

(I, pp. 60–1.)

The quality he observed in Wordsworth's poetry which led to this conclusion was its great difference from the poetry of their contemporaries and of eighteenth-century poets in general. What impressed him in Wordsworth's poetry was

the union of deep feeling with profound thought; the fine balance of

C

truth in observing, with the imaginative faculty in modifying, the objects observed; and above all the original gift of spreading the tone, the atmosphere, and with it the depth and height of the ideal world around forms, incidents and situations, of which, for the common view, custom had bedimmed all the lustre, had dried up the sparkle and the dew drops.

(I, p. 59.)

This gift of Wordsworth's was so pronounced that it led Coleridge to analyse it more fully and to seek an explanation for its originality.

Coleridge's quest finally brought him to the conclusion that eighteenth-century verse was the product of an age which had been taught to think about the imagination in the wrong way and that this misconception had influenced poetic practice. When he first met Wordsworth, Coleridge still belonged to the philosophical tradition of Locke and Hartley, for in December, 1794, he had written to Southey,

I am a compleat Necessitarian – and understand the subject as well almost as Hartley himself – but I go farther than Hartley and believe the corporeality of *thought*, – namely, that it is motion.

(*Collected Letters*, I, p. 137.)

In 1796 he gave his first-born son the name of Hartley, but by this time his reading was taking him back to those writers of the seventeenth century we discussed in the first chapter. We know that Coleridge borrowed Cudworth's *True Intellectual System* from the Bristol Library in the summer of 1795 and again in the autumn of 1796, and we have seen that this would have introduced him to a philosophy which gave an account of the human mind quite different from that of eighteenth-century empiricism. It was Cudworth and the other Platonists who led him to make a distinction which was to become fundamental to his theory of the imagination, for in Chapter X of *Biographia Literaria* he writes, 'I have cautiously discriminated the terms, the reason and the understanding, encouraged and confirmed by the authority of our genuine divines and philosophers, before the Revolution [i.e. of 1688].' Coleridge's reading also extended to earlier neo-Platonic writers such as Plotinus, Proclus and Gemistus Pletho, and embraced the seventeenth-century mystics George Fox and Jacob Boehme, and Boehme's English disciple, William Law. Such writers had become unfashionable in Coleridge's own day, but he tells us in Chapter IX of *Biographia Literaria*, that they 'contributed to keep alive the heart in the head', that they gave him 'an indistinct, yet stirring and working presentiment, that all the products of the mere reflective faculty partook of death'. They were, he tells us, 'always a pillar of fire throughout the night' which had fallen on his soul after becoming disillusioned with Hartley.

Indeed, between the years 1796 and 1801, Coleridge's thought underwent a dramatic change. From being a follower of Hartley and a materialist, he became convinced that the whole tradition of empiricism was wrong in its conception of the human mind. We find him in March, 1801, writing to Thomas Poole of Nether Stowey, that he has 'overthrown the doctrine of Association, as taught by Hartley', and that the attempt to explain mental processes in terms of matter in motion is wrong because it conceives the mind as passive. He sees this as a misplaced application of Newtonian science:

Newton was a mere materialist – *Mind* in his system is always passive – a lazy *looker-on* on an external World. If the mind be not *passive*, if it be indeed made in God's Image, and that, too, in the sublimest sense – the Image of the *Creator* – there is ground for suspicion, that any system built on the passiveness of the mind must be false as a system.

(*Collected Letters*, II, p. 709.)

This disenchantment with Hartley and the tradition of philosophy to which he belonged is fully chronicled in *Biographia*

Literaria. Five chapters of the book are devoted to his growing dissatisfaction with an intellectual system which seemed to him to turn not only the world of nature but the human mind itself into a machine. It was to Platonism that he turned for a more attractive alternative, or as his brother-in-law, Southey, put it in a letter dated July, 1808, 'Hartley was ousted by Berkeley, Berkeley by Spinoza, Spinoza by Plato.'[1] In the later writings of Berkeley he would have found the Christian and neo-Platonic notion that nature is the language of God. According to Berkeley, to be is to be perceived, and all things exist as ideas in God's mind. When we apprehend natural objects we are in touch with God himself, for the natural world is an expression of these divine ideas. Coleridge borrowed the works of Berkeley from the Bristol Library in 1796, and in the following year he incorporated this doctrine in the *Destiny of Nations*:

> All that meets the bodily sense I deem
> Symbolical, one mighty alphabet
> To infant minds; and we in this low world
> Placed with our backs to bright reality,
> That we might learn with young unwounded ken
> The substance from the shadow.

He uses it again in *Frost At Midnight*, written in 1798, where he addresses his infant son, Hartley. He speaks to the child of his own upbringing at Christ's Hospital.

> In the great city, pent 'mid cloisters dim,

and promises the boy a life of freedom and one closer to nature than his own had been:

> so shalt thou see and hear
> The lovely shapes and sounds intelligible
> Of that eternal language, which thy God
> Utters, who from eternity doth teach

[1] Quoted by J. D. Campbell in his *Life* of Coleridge.

> Himself in all, and all things in himself.
> Great universal Teacher! he shall mould
> Thy spirit, and by giving make it ask.

Again Coleridge acknowledged his intellectual allegiance by giving his second son, who was born this year, the name of Berkeley.

Coleridge's interest in Spinoza's philosophy seems to have developed a little later. There was a story current in the family circle that Mrs Coleridge, when about to give birth to a third child, was disconcerted to find her husband immersed in his writings. If there is any truth in this story it would put the date at 1800, for this was the year when the next child, christened Derwent, was born. By this time Coleridge had settled with his family at Keswick. In 1798, after seeing *Lyrical Ballads* in the press, he had left the West Country for a year's stay in Germany, accompanied by William and Dorothy Wordsworth. These dates are of some importance in charting Coleridge's intellectual progress for it has often been suggested that his theory of imagination was derived from his study of German philosophers, especially Kant and Schelling. It is true that in *Biographia Literaria* Coleridge acknowledges his indebtedness to these German writers. He pays tribute to Kant whose writings, he says, 'took possession of me as with the giant's hand', and 'more than any other work, at once invigorated and disciplined my understanding'. (I, p. 99.) He also writes at some length of Schelling, but he insists in 'self-defence against the charge of plagiarism' that 'the most striking resemblances, indeed all the main and fundamental ideas, were born and matured in my mind before I had ever seen a single page of the German Philosopher' (I, p. 102). Coleridge repeated this claim some years later in a letter dated the 8th April, 1825, to his nephew, John Taylor Coleridge, in which he denies that his philosophy is simply a rendering into English of German idealism.

> I can not only honestly assert, but I can satisfactorily prove by reference to writings (Letters, Marginal Notes, and those in books that

have never been in my possession since I first left England for Hamburgh, etc.) that all the elements, the *differentials*, as the algebraists say, of my present opinions existed for me before I had ever seen a book of German Metaphysics, later than Wolf and Leibnitz, or could have read it, if I had.

(*Letters*, II, pp. 735–6.)

There is no reason to doubt Coleridge's word in this matter. He was quite ready to acknowledge his debt to the Germans and, in any case, as he declared in *Biographia Literaria*, he regarded 'truth as a divine ventriloquist: I care not from whose mouth the sounds are supposed to proceed, if only the words were audible and intelligible' (I, p. 105). The Germans gave his thought greater coherence and, as far as his theory of the imagination was concerned, they enabled him to fit this into a comprehensive philosophical system. Even so, from what we know of his reading, his Notebooks, and his correspondence before his visit to Germany, it is manifestly possible that he had worked out for himself an alternative to the empiricist philosophy of the eighteenth century. As we have seen, his starting point was the conviction that Wordsworth's poetic genius derived from a power which could not be explained by the association of ideas. In other words, his concern was with the imagination, and this is why the history of his intellectual development in *Biographia Literaria* culminates in the famous description of the imagination in Chapter XIII. In this part of his philosophy there is good ground for believing that he had worked out his views before he was able to read German. No doubt Kant and Schelling were to contribute to the formulation of his theory, but there were, as we shall see, some respects in which there remained differences between them.

What Coleridge gained from his reading of the English Platonists (including the later Berkeley) was the conviction that associationism was a too facile account of the mental processes involved in imagination and in how the mind perceives and knows.

Furthermore, it led him to believe that any account of nature as simply matter in motion was unsatisfactory. In both respects it provided more acceptable alternatives, but even more than this, the Platonists indicated how the two principles concerned with mind and nature might be related. For over against the view that the mind is passive in perception they taught that the mind is partly an architect of its own knowledge, that there is a reciprocity between nature and the mind of man. Cudworth especially, among the Cambridge Platonists, pointed out that there is more in human perception than what is given by the senses. He takes the example of a house or palace and declares that

> The eye or sense of a brute, though it have as much passively impressed upon it from without as the soul of a man hath, . . . could not comprehend from thence the formal idea and nature of a house or palace, which nothing but an active intellectual principle can reach into.

> *(True Intellectual System,* III, p. 594.)

Cudworth proceeds from this example to suggest that the same is true of the whole of nature. What we know of the world through our senses is a disordered mass of discrete entities, whereas the mind imposes an order and unity upon the world. He illustrates this by drawing an analogy with music and takes the argument further by maintaining that the order and unity we perceive in nature derive from 'one infinite and eternal mind as containing the plot of the whole mundane music'. But even if religious belief were left out of the argument, there would still remain the difference between human perception and sensation. The ancients, wrote Cudworth,

> made Pan, that is nature, to play upon a harp; but sense which only passively receives particular outward objects doth here, like the brute, hear nothing but mere noise and sound and clatter, but no music or harmony at all; having no active principle and anticipation within itself to comprehend it by, and correspond or vitally sympathize with

it; whereas the mind of a rational and intellectual being will be ravished and enthusiastically transported in the contemplation of it and of its own accordance to this pipe of Pan, nature's intellectual music and harmony.

(*Op. cit.*, III, p. 600.)

In a chapter on Cudworth in *The Platonic Tradition in Anglo-Saxon Philosophy* (New York, 1900), J. H. Muirhead quotes the above passages and, in a footnote, observes that they remind us of 'Coleridge's view of Nature, and the theory of art which he based upon it'. 'What must always seem strange,' he adds, 'is that he should have had to go to Schelling for a doctrine that was staring him in the face in his own Cambridge predecessors.' The truth, of course, is that Coleridge was well aware of Cudworth; indeed, in one important respect Schelling went further than either Coleridge or Cudworth was prepared to go. Schelling's philosophy was pantheistic, whereas Coleridge was never in any real sense a pantheist; he believed that nature symbolized a transcendental reality but not that it was identical with it. There are several references in Coleridge's writings to his disagreement not only with Schelling, but also Spinoza, on the subject of pantheism. *The Eolian Harp*, is often cited as an expression of his so-called pantheism, but this poem was written between August and October, 1795, just after he had been reading the *True Intellectual System*, and the following well-known lines may echo the passage from Cudworth quoted above:

> Or what if all of animated nature
> Be but organic Harps diversely fram'd,
> That tremble into thought, as o'er them sweeps
> Plastic and vast, one intellectual breeze,
> At once the Soul of each, and God of all?

In the poem Coleridge imagines his newly-wedded bride gently rebuking him for such thoughts, but this could well be not so much for any real unorthodoxy as for her dislike of metaphysical speculation about religion. He may, indeed, simply be anticipating what he later expressed in a letter of 10th September, 1802, to William Sotheby, in which he contrasts the Greek religious poets with the Hebrew poets of the Old Testament. The Greek writers, he says, were poets of fancy, whereas the Hebrew poets wrote with the power of imagination. The important point here is that Coleridge advances again what could be mistaken for pantheism, if it were not for the Biblical language he uses:

> In the Hebrew Poets each Thing has a Life of its own, and yet they are all one Life. In God they move and live, and *have* their Being – not *had*, as the cold system of Newtonian Theology represents – but *have*.

> (*Collected Letters*, II, p. 866.)

For Coleridge, as for Cudworth, there was a parallelism between a vitalistic conception of nature and a view of the mind as creative in knowledge. As God created the world out of Chaos and gave it order and form, so the human mind imposes order and form upon the raw material of sensation. The human mind can do this because it is made in the image of the Divine Mind and is truly creative. The world was not created by God in one determinate act and left by Him to run in accordance with Newtonian laws; it is sustained in being by the spirit of God and is, in a phrase Coleridge was fond of using, *natura naturans* and not *natura naturata*. So, by analogy though in a very real sense, the human mind creates the world it perceives, and because this is possible, there must be a reciprocity between the world of perception and the faculties of the mind. In this way Coleridge resolved a problem with which he had struggled from the beginning: how thought can come to terms with things. The power which enables us to relate the two worlds of mind and nature is the imagination. In Chapter XIII of *Biographia Literaria* he calls it 'a repetition in the finite mind of the eternal act of creation in the infinite I AM', but as far back as 1801, in the letter to Thomas Poole from which we have already quoted, he speaks of the human mind as made in 'the *Image of the Creator*', and in a letter to Richard Sharp, in January, 1804, he describes the imagination as 'a dim analogue of creation'.

So far then, Coleridge had begun to elaborate a theory of the imagination which was concerned with perception, with how the mind embraces the world of objects which it half creates and half perceives. But this process of creation applies to art as well as to nature. Indeed, the generally accepted view of the poetic imagination as memory images brought together by association might explain a certain type of poetry, but it did nothing to explain poetry of the highest kind. And so Coleridge began to distinguish between the poetry of talent and the poetry of genius in terms of the fancy and the imagination. Fancy is an associative process; the imagination is a creative one. Just as in perception the imagination imposes form and order upon the material of sensation and half creates what it perceives, so in art it works upon the raw material of experience, giving it a new form and shape. To do this it must first break down the material before it can recreate it, for the imagination is not a mirror but a creative principle. The artistic imagination creates a new world; one like the everyday world of perception, but reorganized and raised to a higher level of universality. In Chapter XIV of *Biographia Literaria* Coleridge quotes from the poem *Nosce Teipsum*, by the Elizabethan poet, Sir John Davies, to illustrate this creative activity of the poetic imagination. The poem describes how the mind derives knowledge from sense objects,

> As fire converts to fire the thing it burns,
> As we our food into our nature change.

But, as Coleridge says, the 'words may with slight alteration be applied; and even more appropriately, to the poetic IMAGINA-TION', for the stanzas which follow refer not only to the apprehension of the essences of things but to the process of recreating them in sensible form:

From their gross matter she abstracts their forms,
    And draws a kind of quintessence from things;
Which to her proper nature she transforms
    To bear them light on her celestial wings.

Thus doth she, when from individual states
    She doth abstract the universal kinds;
Which then re-clothed in divers names and fates
    Steal access through our senses to our minds.

We can now understand the distinction between fancy and imagination which Coleridge elaborates in Chapter XIII of *Biographia Literaria*. The fancy he tells us 'is indeed no other than a mode of memory emancipated from the order of time and space'. It receives 'all its materials ready made from the law of association'. It is clear that by fancy he means what had generally been accepted as a total account of the imaginative process by the eighteenth-century empiricists. But he is anxious to distinguish this from what he believes to be the real imagination. The imagination proper, he tells us, can be considered 'either as primary, or secondary'. The primary imagination is that faculty which mediates between sensation and perception. It is 'the living power and prime agent of all human perception', and 'a repetition in the finite mind of the eternal act of creation in the infinite I AM'. This faculty is operative in all of us for we are all percipient beings whether we like it or not. He then proceeds to give his description of the secondary or poetic imagination. This is

> . . . an echo of the former, co-existing with the conscious will, yet still as identical with the primary in the *kind* of its agency, and differing only in *degree*, and in the *mode* of its operation. It dissolves, diffuses, dissipates, in order to re-create: or where this process is rendered impossible, yet still at all events it struggles to idealize and to unify.
>
> (I, p. 202.)

The essential difference between the primary and the secondary imagination is that the one is involuntary, for we cannot choose whether to perceive or not, whereas the other is related to 'the conscious will'. Another difference is that the secondary imagination cannot always achieve the unity it seeks and is not always entirely successful in its struggle to unify. But like the primary imagination, the secondary is a creative process. 'It is essentially *vital*, even as all objects (*as* objects) are essentially fixed and dead.' In this respect the poetic imagination is unlike the fancy which 'on the contrary, has no other counters to play with, but fixities and definites'.

In all important respects this does not differ from the neo-Platonic description of how the mind apprehends reality which is given in Sir John Davies's poem. The mind perceives in and through sense objects the eternal forms of things and has the power to represent these Platonic Ideas in an imaginary or fictional guise. This would explain Coleridge's use of the word 'idealize' in the passage quoted above. It is often asked by what principle Coleridge's poetic imagination operates. If it is not merely to reproduce the world of everyday perception, then there must be some ideal which it seeks to approximate, and if so, what is this ideal? Coleridge's answer to this question might seem to be that the poetic imagination strives to show us what is 'really real', the structure of the universe, the basic stuff of human experience, the reality behind appearances, or something of the kind indicated by such phrases. But all he tells us in this passage is that the poetic imagination 'struggles to idealize and to unify'.

It becomes clear in reading the *Biographia Literaria* that Coleridge's theory of the imagination owes something both to Platonism and to the philosophy of Kant and his followers, and one of the difficulties in understanding his theory is that maybe he never reconciles the two. There is good reason for believing that

Coleridge tried to Platonise Kant and this would be natural enough for someone who approached German philosophy after steeping himself in Platonism.[1]

Certainly in *Biographia Literaria*, and even more so in his later writings, we have to relate what he says about the imagination to both Kant and Schelling. This is evident in Chapter VII of *Biographia Literaria* where he is writing about 'the mind's self-experience in the act of thinking' and continues,

> There are evidently two powers at work, which relatively to each other are active and passive; and this is not possible without an intermediate faculty, which is at once both active and passive. (In philosophical language, we must denominate this intermediate faculty in all its degrees and determinations, the IMAGINATION.)
>
> (I, p. 86.)

The context makes it clear that Coleridge regards the imagination as mediating not only between sensation and perception, but also between perception and thought. The primary imagination enables us not only to perceive objects but also to frame concepts and to engage in discursive thinking. Furthermore, in Chapter IX of *Biographia Literaria*, where he is discussing the secondary imagination, he declares that

[1] In one respect, however, there was an irreconcilable difference between Plato and Kant and this was in moral philosophy. There is an interesting MS note in Coleridge's copy of Thomas Taylor's *The Philosophical and Mathematical Commentaries of Proclus . . . and a History of Platonic Philosophy by the latter Platonists* (1792), in which he recognizes this difference and equates Kant as a moralist with Zeno, the founder of the Stoic school, but in other respects sees Kant as a modern Plato. 'It seems clear', the note reads,

> that the Critical Philosophy, as contained in the works of Immanuel Kantius, is a Junction of the Stoic *Moral* with the Platonic *Dialectic* . . . which is in truth the same with his own transcendental Logic.

The note is reprinted in Appendix B of *The Notebooks of S. T. Coleridge*, Vol. I, ed. Kathleen Coburn, 1957. Miss Coburn writes of Coleridge's study of Kant that it probably began 'about 1801–2, though more intensive study came I suspect in 1803, again after 1810, and more still after 1817, i.e. between the composition of the *Biographia* and the 1818 *Friend*.' (*Ibid.*, 1517.)

An IDEA in the *highest* sense of the word cannot be conveyed but by a symbol.

(I, p. 100.)

Here the imagination is seen as mediating between the understanding, which is concerned with conceptualization, and the reason, which is concerned with a knowledge that transcends concepts. In this chapter he is discussing Kant and recognizes a certain identity between their views.

Kant distinguishes three kinds or levels of imagination. The first is the reproductive imagination and is very much what Coleridge means by fancy. Next there is the productive imagination, which corresponds to Coleridge's primary imagination; it operates between sense perception and the understanding and enables the latter to carry on its work of discursive reasoning. It is the bridge which links the world of thought and the world of things. Finally, there is what Kant calls the aesthetic imagination; this is productive, too, but is free of the laws which govern the understanding, for it is not tied to the world of sense experience. The aesthetic imagination serves not the understanding but the reason, which furnishes the mind with Ideas, that is with principles above sensory knowledge and empirical verification. The reason provides these principles which are necessary to order and explain experience but are not themselves explained by it. In the Kantian analysis there are two kinds of Ideas. One of these consists of Rational Ideas, which Kant describes as 'transcendent concepts'; they are conceptual in form, but unlike the concepts of the understanding, they cannot be verified by experience. The other, and this is the province of art, consists of Aesthetic Ideas. An Aesthetic Idea is like a Rational Idea in going beyond and yet being necessary to explain experience, but it differs from a Rational Idea by being non-conceptual. It is, indeed, what we would call a symbol, though not in the sense of an arbitrary or conventional sign. No concept is able to express the total content of the symbol for, as Kant explains, it is a

. . . representation of the imagination which induces much thought, yet without the possibility of any definite thought whatever, i.e. *concept*, being adequate to it, and which language, consequently, can never get quite on level terms with or render completely intelligible.

(*Critique of Judgement*, trans. Meredith, Oxford, 1911, pp. 175–6.)

The aesthetic imagination mediates, then, between the reason and the understanding by means of symbols. The understanding furnishes conceptual knowledge to the reason, and the reason in turn stimulates the understanding to further thought by a reciprocity between concept and symbol. It follows from this analysis that there is much in thought which cannot be expressed exactly in language. Moreover, the meaning of a work of art is inexhaustible in that the understanding will frame concept after concept in an attempt to explain it and yet never be wholly successful. To use a fine phrase of T. S. Eliot's in *Four Quartets*, poetry is 'a raid upon the inarticulate', and the critical commentary upon a poem is never-ending.

There is much in *Biographia Literaria* which would support this kind of interpretation of Coleridge's theory of imagination, but his use of the word 'Idea' still carries something of a Platonic rather than a Kantian meaning. For Kant's Ideas were not like Plato's, they were concerned only with the phenomenal and not with what Kant called the noumenal or 'things in themselves'. Coleridge did not accept this Kantian limitation of the reason and even found it difficult to believe that Kant himself did.

In spite therefore of his own declaration, I could never believe, that it was possible for him to have meant no more by his *Noumenon*, or THING IN ITSELF, than his mere words express; or that in his own conception he confined the whole *plastic* power to the forms of the intellect, leaving for the external cause, for the *materiale* of our sensations, a matter without form, which is doubtless inconceivable.

(I, p. 100.)

The point is of some importance for aesthetic theory, since the Kantian viewpoint sees art as the representation of an idea in the artist's mind, whereas the neo-Platonic sees it as the representation of reality itself. Under the influence of Schelling, Coleridge tried to bring these two viewpoints together. Indeed it was Schelling's identification of nature and mind, and the notion of the imagination as the means of achieving or recognizing this identity, which first attracted Coleridge to him. But Coleridge's Christian conviction led him to realize that the identification left no place for a transcendent God and he rejected Schelling as he had rejected Boehme before, and for the same reason. In a letter of the 24th November, 1818, he wrote about Schelling's philosophy:

. . . as a *System*, it is little more than Behmenism, translated from visions into Logic and a sort of commanding eloquence: and like Behmen's it is reduced at last to a mere Pantheism.[1]

In *The Statesman's Manual* (1816) Coleridge attempted to modify his philosophy to overcome this kind of objection, but our concern is with the literary imagination and we must leave this out of our consideration.

Biographia Literaria is a sketch of Coleridge's *literary* life and opinions and although it contains a lengthy excursion into philosophy we should not forget this. Some writers have criticized the work for a lack of unity and fail to recognize any relationship between the first half, which traces the course of Coleridge's thought, and the second, which is taken up with a discussion of poetry and mainly Wordsworth's poetry at that. It is true that the thread of Coleridge's thought is sometimes lost to view in the digressions he makes in his argument, but this should not lead us to think his work lacks unity. There are those who see no connexion between philosophical principles and literary criticism, but to

[1] *Collected Letters*, IV, p. 883. Coleridge generally used the form *Behmen* for Boehme.

deny this connexion is to deny the possibility of philosophical criticism and this, of course, was Coleridge's main concern. He sees 'the ultimate end of criticism' as 'much more to establish the principles of writing than to furnish *rules* how to pass judgement on what has been written by others' (II, p. 63), and his own criticism provides impressive evidence of the relevance of this to the critic's task.

Biographia Literaria begins with an account of the author's early taste in literature and the influence upon him of Bowles's poetry, but it is not long before we come to Wordsworth and their joint venture in poetry which had been published as *Lyrical Ballads*. Wordsworth had explained the nature of their poetic experiments in a short *Advertisement* to the first edition of 1798, and had defended the poems against the criticism levelled against them in a lengthy *Preface* to the 1800 edition, and again in a modified version of this in the 1802 edition. Later, Wordsworth wrote another Preface, this time to the 1815 edition of his *Poems*, in which he made his own distinction between the fancy and the imagination and illustrated it by a discussion of his own poetry and that of Shakespeare and Milton. Wordsworth's distinction is not so precise as Coleridge's and in some ways even runs counter to it. As an example of this, Wordsworth, writes:

> Fancy, as she is an active, is also, under her own laws and in her own spirit, a creative faculty. In what manner Fancy ambitiously aims at a rivalship with Imagination, and Imagination stoops to work with the materials of Fancy, might be illustrated from the compositions of all eloquent writers, whether in prose or verse; and chiefly from those of our own Country.

In *Biographia Literaria* Coleridge expresses his disagreement with Wordsworth:

> I shall now proceed to the nature and genesis of the imagination; but I must first take leave to notice, that after a more accurate perusal of

D

Mr Wordsworth's remarks on the imagination, in his preface to the new edition of his poems, I find that my conclusions are not so consentient with his as, I confess, I had taken for granted.

(I, p. 193.)

He also feels that Wordsworth's earlier Prefaces had hindered an appreciation of the poetic revolution they had both laboured to bring about.

In the critical remarks, therefore, prefixed and annexed to the *Lyrical Ballads*, I believe that we may safely rest, as the true origin of the unexampled opposition which Mr Wordsworth's writings have been since doomed to encounter.

(I, p. 51.)

He follows this later with a more explicit expression of his disagreement with Wordsworth:

With many parts of this preface in the sense attributed to them, and which the words undoubtedly seem to authorize, I never concurred; but on the contrary objected to them as erroneous in principle, and as contradictory . . . to the author's own practice in the greater number of the poems themselves.

(II, pp. 7–8.)

This dissatisfaction with Wordsworth's defence of their poetic endeavours goes right back to the time when the original Preface to *Lyrical Ballads* was written, for on the 13th July, 1802, Coleridge wrote to his friend Sotheby, '. . . the f[irst pass]ages were indeed partly taken from notes of mine', but, he adds, '. . . we begin to suspect, that there is, somewhere or other, a *radical* Difference [in our] opinions' (*Collected Letters*, II, p. 811). It is not difficult to detect the source of Coleridge's dissatisfaction, for a good deal of Wordsworth's Preface was written in the language of Hartley. Indeed, 'the principal object' of the poems, according to Wordsworth, was to trace, 'the primary laws of our nature: chiefly as far as regards the manner in which we associate ideas in a state of excitement'. By this time Coleridge was already disillusioned with Hartley, and no doubt it was Coleridge who prompted Wordsworth to include in the revised Preface of 1802 a long passage on the question, 'What is a Poet?', which approximates more closely to his own views.

The nature of Wordsworth's genius was one he found it difficult to explain in intellectual terms. His poetic vision was, perhaps, a more personal one than Coleridge realized; but Coleridge thought that he could understand and analyse it for he had stood closer to Wordsworth than any other critic and, in spite of their differences, he felt he had shared this vision. The unity of *Biographia Literaria* consists, then, in its analysis of the poetic imagination and its discussion of Wordsworth's poetry as an illustration of the imagination at work. In many ways it can be viewed as the belated Preface to *Lyrical Ballads*, which at first Coleridge had thought of writing, but which had been left to Wordsworth.

With this in mind we realize that there is no lack of continuity between Chapter XIII of *Biographia Literaria* in which Coleridge sets out his distinction between the fancy and the imagination, and Chapter XIV in which he asks 'What is poetry?' The poet 'in ideal perfection', he tells us, in the passage quoted at the beginning of this chapter, 'diffuses a tone and spirit of unity' and achieves this by the exercise of his imagination. The unity is brought about by

> the balance or reconciliation of opposite or discordant qualities; of sameness, with difference; of the general, with the concrete; the idea, with the image; the individual, with the representative; the sense of novelty and freshness, with old and familiar objects; a more than usual state of emotion, with more than usual order; judgement ever awake and steady self-possession, with enthusiasm and feeling profound or vehement.
>
> (II, p. 12.)

This is in accordance with his earlier statement that '. . . all symbols of necessity involve an apparent contradiction' (I, p. 100). They will be contradictory because they were partly object and partly thought; individual and yet representative; both image and idea. But above all, they will bring together what he considered the two cardinal principles of great poetry, 'truth to nature' and 'the interest of novelty'. This theoretical analysis was confirmed empirically by Wordsworth's poetry, which more than any other combined the truth of natural description with novelty and freshness. Wordsworth had taken the objects of everyday perception, a 'known and familiar landscape' or 'characters and incidents . . . found in every village and its vicinity', and by investing them with 'the modifying colours of imagination', had transformed them into symbols of universal truth. The novelty of Wordsworth's poetry springs from the freshness of his vision which can both see and communicate this universal character in the ordinary and familiar. His genius is essentially the power of taking what 'custom had bedimmed' and endowing it with 'the depth and height of the ideal world'.

Having said this, Coleridge was compelled to recognize that not all of Wordsworth's poetry was at this imaginative level. There was, in certain poems, what he called 'a *matter-of-factness*', a liking for the detailed and even the accidental. This was the product not of the imagination, but of an aggregating process which was no more than fancy. There is, too, a logical connexion between this and Coleridge's strictures on Wordsworth's style and language in some of the poems, for language is above all the mediating factor which links the world of nature and the world of thought. In places Wordsworth's language had failed to produce a satisfactory unity between the two. So although Coleridge claims for his friend 'the gift of Imagination in the highest and strictest sense of the word', he has to admit that 'In the play of *fancy*, Wordsworth . . . is not always graceful'; his use of fancy appears 'the creature of predetermined research, rather than spontaneous presentation'. Nevertheless, Coleridge had no doubt that in Wordsworth he had known a poetic genius who 'stands nearest of all modern writers to Shake-speare and Milton; and yet in a kind perfectly unborrowed and his own'. His own words, declares Coleridge, 'are at once an instance and an illustration, he does indeed to all thoughts and to all objects

> add the gleam,
> The light that never was, on sea or land,
> The consecration, and the poet's dream'.

(II, p. 124.)

3
Symbol and Concept

The key to Coleridge's critical theory is his notion of symbol. For him, a work of art is a symbol which mediates between the world of nature and the world of thought. The act of aesthetic appreciation as well as the act of artistic creation is a symbolization of experience achieved through the power of the imagination. But what value, it may be asked, has this for the practice of criticism? Coleridge himself believed that it has value and not only for the critic but the poet as well. The distinction between the fancy and the imagination, and this implies a doctrine of symbolism,

> ... would in its immediate effects furnish a torch of guidance to the philosophical critic; and ultimately to the poet himself. In energetic minds, truth soon changes by domestication into power; and from directing in the discrimination and appraisal of the product, becomes influencive in the production.

(II, p. 62.)

Coleridge never believed his theory would give the critic a set of rules which he could apply to a work of art and decide by their application that it was, or was not, a work of genius. Indeed, his theory specifically excludes this, and one of his achievements, historically speaking, was to deliver criticism from any vestiges of the neo-classical rules which remained at the end of the eighteenth century. For him every work of art is unique and although he recognizes the existence of literary *genres*, these have come into being, not by arbitrary decree but because of the nature of the material they embody. The task of the critic is not to observe how closely a work of art approximates to a formal definition, but to discern how fully it realizes the laws implicit in its own nature. This nature is organic and not mechanical; the one great principle is to discern and trace in a work its growth, how the elements come together and form a unity which is more than the sum of the individual parts. This organic unity is an essential feature of what Coleridge means by a symbol.

Symbol for him stands over against concept, but it is by the interaction of the two that the human mind reaches its highest achievements. The mind will endeavour to express the significance of its own experience in symbolic forms for conceptual expression is often inadequate. But the conceptualizing understanding will always seek to interpret the symbols of art even when it realizes that the attempt can never be wholly successful. The task of the artist is to embody his experience in symbols, but the task of the critic is the attempt to translate these into discursive thought. Art then will use the objects of the natural world to express its vision of things; criticism will endeavour to judge how successful the achievement has been. The critic will first ask himself whether the poet has simply translated thought into the language of poetry – a charge Coleridge levelled at Pope – or whether he has embodied his thought in symbols which match the thought so exactly that the symbols and the thought they symbolize are virtually inseparable. For this reason Coleridge distinguished symbol from allegory. 'The symbolical', he wrote,

> cannot, perhaps, be better defined in distinction from the Allegorical, than that it is always itself a part of that, of the whole of which it is the representative.
>
> (*Coleridge's Miscellaneous Criticism*, ed. J. M. Raysor, p. 99.)

The same kind of distinction is implicit in Coleridge's comparison in *The Statesman's Manual* between the imaginative treatment of historical figures in the Old Testament and the lifeless abstractions of contemporary historians. The latter, he says, 'partake in the general contagion of its mechanistic philosophy'. The former, on the other hand.

> . . . are living *educts* of the Imagination; of that reconciling and mediatory power, which incorporating the Reason in Images of the Sense . . . gives birth to a system of symbols, harmonious in themselves, and consubstantial with the truths, of which they are the *conductors*.

The Old Testament characters are not allegorical figures, they are what Coleridge describes as both 'Portraits and Ideals'.

The same is true of Shakespeare's dramatic characters, according to Coleridge, for they, too, show the power of genius or imagination, which fuses together the observation of men and women and the transcendent quality of the poet's own mind. Shakespeare's imagination is, for Coleridge, a fusion of the objective and the subjective. His characters are not drawn from life in the sense that they are amalgams of particular individuals; they are created 'by the simple force of meditation'.

> Shakespeare's characters, from Othello and Macbeth down to Dogberry and the Grave-digger, may be termed ideal realities. They are not the things themselves, so much as abstracts of the things, which a great mind takes into itself, and there naturalizes them to its own conception.
>
> (*Shakespearean Criticism*, ed. T. M. Raysor, II, p. 125, Everyman's Library, 1960.)

This paradox is explicable only in terms of a mediating power such as the imagination, which enables the poet of genius to assimilate the outside world into his own consciousness and make it a symbolic representation of his own mind. Coleridge refers to this kind of subjective universality which characterized Shakespeare above all, when he describes in *Biographia Literaria* how Shakespeare 'darts himself forth, and passes into all the forms of human character and passion ... [and] becomes all things, yet forever remaining himself' (II, p. 20). Milton, though a genius, was more subjective than Shakespeare, for he 'is himself before himself in everything he writes', whereas 'Shakespeare is universal, and, in fact, has no *manner*' (*Table Talk*, pp. 93 and 213). In even greater contrast to Shakespeare, the Elizabethan dramatists display in their work 'mere aggregations without unity' (as in Beaumont and Fletcher) or 'an amassing power ... and not ... a growth from within' (as in Ben Jonson). These were poets of fancy and not imagination, they

> ... took from the ear and eye, unchecked by any intuition of an inward possibility, just as a man might fit together a quarter of an orange, a quarter of an apple, and the like of a lemon and of a pomegranate, and make it look like one round diverse coloured fruit.
>
> (*Miscellaneous Criticism*, pp. 44–47.)

They had no forming idea in the mind which created and controlled their work, but were content to select and assemble the elements in accordance with the external laws of literary *genres* or contemporary taste.

It is difficult to see why some writers have maintained that Coleridge's theory of imagination is irrelevant to the task of criticism, for he taught us to look at literature in a new way. Indeed, it could be argued that symbolism as a critical principle has become too pervasive since his time and led critics away from other ways of looking at literature. This is true, perhaps, especially in drama, where his speculation caused criticism both to concentrate on character rather than dramatic action and, even more, to neglect dramatic and theatrical considerations in favour of looking at plays as if they were simply poems. Nevertheless, in his own practice as a critic Coleridge did more than view a dramatic work as simply a symbolic expression of thought. In his Lectures on Shakespeare he used the notion to provide a critical procedure by which he examines the plays in terms of his own balance or reconciliation of opposites. He explains the opposition between high and low life and characters, for instance, as one which leads to a more compelling synthesis, as one which does not destroy unity but creates it.

Coleridge is eager to combat the notion that Shakespeare's genius is irrational and to dispel the picture of him as a 'child of nature' or an 'unbridled genius'. This was a central concern in all the Lectures he gave on Shakespeare, of which he wrote,

> ... it has been and still remains my object to prove that in all points from the most important to the most minute, the judgement of Shakespeare is commensurate with his genius – nay, that his genius reveals itself in his judgement, as in its most exalted form.
>
> (*Shakespearean Criticism*, I, p. 114.)

This is important for understanding not only his criticism of Shakespeare but his analysis of the imagination. We have seen already that Coleridge calls the imagination 'the agent of the reason', and that it operates under the direction of the will. Indeed, one can regard it as an instrument of knowledge, for the great poet is also a philosopher, who interprets experience not, it is true, in logical terms, but in the symbolic structures of art which are analogues of the metaphysical systems of the abstract thinker. The interplay of symbol and concept, too, is one which advances man's knowledge of himself and the world he inhabits. This raises two questions which we have not yet faced. The first is, what part do the feelings play in Coleridge's theory; is the imagination a purely rational faculty? The second is, what relation is there between the imagination and the world of dreams and the unconscious? Both questions are of some significance in the development given to his thought by later generations.

The answer to the first of these questions is fairly straightforward. It would be a mistake to regard terms such as reason and understanding, fancy and imagination, as entities; they are not so much faculties as processes. Coleridge was emphatic in his insistence that the human mind is like an organism and not a machine. His observations on Hartley's theory of vibrations are as relevant today, when attempts have been made to describe the brain in terms of a computer, as they were when he made them; and his refusal to identify nerve impulses with consciousness is still valid as a criticism of behaviourist psychology. It is true that his concentration on epistemology in the *Biographia Literaria* leads him to say little about the emotions, but throughout his writings we become aware of the importance he attaches to them, and in the portrait of the poet in Chapter XIV of the *Biographia Literaria* he writes of the union of 'judgement ever awake and steady self-possession with enthusiasm and feeling profound or vehement'. The feelings undoubtedly play their part, and strong feelings at that, but they are always at the command of artistic control. The idea is a harmony which 'brings the whole soul of man into activity', but the emotions have their place in this harmony.

But, ask some commentators, is this theorizing not all an elaborate superstructure raised by Coleridge's interest in metaphysics, when we know all the time that his own poetry was the product of dreams and an inspiration that owed more to opium than to rational ideas? The question of opium may be disposed of fairly quickly. The answer to it, in the simplest terms, lies in the fact that for every poet who has resorted to opium, there must be a thousand other people who have taken opium without being granted the gift of writing poetry. Of course, *Kubla Khan* has given currency to the notion that Coleridge's imagination fed on opium, but in a recent book, *Opium and the Romantic Imagination*, Miss Alethea Hayter puts the matter well when she argues that the poem was composed not in a dream but, to use his own words, 'in a sort of Rêverie brought on by two grains of Opium'. Out of this kind of rêverie most addicts, she writes,

... can produce nothing of value ... because they have not got the imagination, the memory, the learning of a Coleridge. He, with his external senses switched off but his mind still awake and able to observe the linked words and images unwinding simultaneously out of itself, was able to produce a draft of what was to become *Kubla Khan*.

(*Op. cit.*, p. 223.)

So, too, with dreams. Coleridge was fascinated by dreams and the unconscious mind and would readily have admitted that the raw material of poetry may come from this other world within ourselves. But he would have insisted that it must be given shape, that it must submit to the control of the artistic judgement, before it can become properly symbolic.

There is another sense, however, in which dream is sometimes related to art. This lies in a metaphorical usage of the kind we find in Keats's letter to Benjamin Bailey, in which he wrote in a famous passage:

I am certain of nothing but of the holiness of the Heart's affections and the truth of Imagination – What the imagination seizes as Beauty must be truth – whether it existed before or not ... The Imagination may be compared to Adam's dream – he awoke and found it truth.

(Letter of 22 Nov. 1817, *Letters of John Keats*, ed. M. B. Forman, 4th edn., p. 67.)

This looks as if it might be an echo of Coleridge and one could be encouraged to detect a similarity in their views by their remarks on Shakespeare; for Coleridge's paradoxical combination of subjectivity and objectivity in assessing the work of Shakespeare is paralleled in Keats's use of the phrase 'innate universality' to characterize his genius.[1] Keats employs a better-known phrase, 'negative capability', to describe this quality he admired in Shake-

---

[1] The phrase was used by Keats in an annotation to an edition of Shakespeare. See *The Life and Letters of Keats* by Lord Houghton (Everyman's Library), p. 94.

speare. This refers to what he regards as Shakespeare's objectivity in representing life truthfully, but free from any final theoretical explanations. For him, Shakespeare's mind was content to rest in doubt and uncertainty; it could represent a comic vision of life as well as a tragic one, without claiming an ultimate validity for either. It is significant that in the letter in which he uses the phrase he should compare this kind of mind with Coleridge's search for certitude:

> *Negative Capability*, that is when a man is capable of being in uncertainties, Mysteries, doubts, without any irritable reaching after fact and reason – Coleridge, for instance, would let go by a fine isolated verisimilitude caught from the Penetralium of mystery, from being incapable of remaining Content with half knowledge.
>
> (Letter of 21 Dec. 1817. *Op. cit.*, p. 71.)

But Keats's conception of the imagination was not the same as Coleridge's. The vision of the poet, Adam's dream, is true only in the sense that it represents life as the poet sees it, at the moment, without any claim to absolute certitude. His great Odes betray a deep, if noble, scepticism about the scope of the imagination. The song of the nightingale is, for Keats, an emblem of poetry and it is significant that his *Ode to a Nightingale* ends not with affirmation but a question:

> Was it a vision, or a waking dream?
> Fled is that music: do I wake or sleep?

The Odes suggest that Keats came increasingly to feel that the imagination was a dream which would vanish with the dawn. Even the *Ode on a Grecian Urn*, with its final affirmation, 'Beauty is truth, truth beauty', expresses this mood. The commentary on this utterance of the urn has been almost endless, but the rest of Keats's writings confirms that what he meant by it was only to suggest that every work of art has its own validity as a representation of reality. In Keats there is no counterpart to the neo-Platonic belief that we catch glimpses in and through the world of our senses of a transcendent reality beyond, and that the poet above others is able to discern and represent this reality; nor is there anything approaching Coleridge's impressive analysis of how we come to have knowledge and the part played by the imagination in this process.

Coleridge did not regard the imagination as a form of intuition which penetrates to the supersensuous Ideas behind the appearance of things; nor, for him, was it an autonomous faculty which guarantees the truth of what it apprehends. No doubt there were elements of both these views in the earlier neo-Platonic stages of his thought, but any such tendency was corrected by Kant and, even before he knew Kant's writings, by Cudworth. Kant explained the imagination in terms of a comprehensive epistemology and Coleridge followed him in this by describing the imagination as operating under the reason. It is true that Coleridge went beyond Kant in believing that the reason could give us more than a knowledge of the world of perception. But it would be wrong to think that Coleridge regarded the imagination as giving us an access to truth beyond the scope of reason. Moreover, the symbols of the imagination have to accommodate themselves to the concepts of the understanding; there is never a conflict in Coleridge's mind between poetry and science or discursive thought. Nor did he think that poetry was a substitute for religion. Reason, in his view, does not supplant faith, but in its practical aspects confirms faith, which must be a matter of personal commitment. The truth of Christianity will declare itself in answering the needs of the human spirit, for as he wrote in the final chapter of *Biographia Literaria*:

> ... this is the seeming argumentum in circulo incidental to all spiritual Truths ... as long as we attempt to master by the reflex acts of the Understanding what we can only *know* by the act of *becoming. Do the will of my Father, and ye shall KNOW whether I am of God.*
>
> (II, p. 216.)

But there were those who made claims for the imagination which went beyond those advanced by Coleridge and which led towards an identification of poetry and religion. Shelley's *Defence of Poetry*, written in 1821, but not published until 1840, is a curious mixture of neo-Platonism and an empiricist psychology. It starts with an attempt to relate the reason and the imagination, but in a manner quite different from Coleridge's. Shelley's essay takes us back to the Judgement–Fancy distinction of Hobbes. 'Reason,' he writes,

> is the enumeration of quantities already known; imagination is the perception of the value of those quantities, both separately and as a whole. Reason respects the differences, and imagination the similitude of things.

But, unlike Hobbes, he sets the imagination above the reason, for, he continues,

> Reason is to imagination as the instrument to the agent, as the body to the spirit, as the shadow to the substance.
>
> (*Shelley's Literary and Philosophical Criticism*, ed. J. Shawcross, 1909, p. 120.)

Against Coleridge, he asserts that poetry

> ... differs in this respect from logic, that it is not subject to the control of the active powers of the mind, and that its birth and recurrence have no necessary connexion with the consciousness or will.
>
> (*Ibid.*, p. 157.)

Imagination, for Shelley, enables the poet to discern the Platonic Ideas which lie behind sensible appearances, and which have at their apex the Idea of the Good. At the end of his *Defence* he promises the reader a second part which will

> ... have for its object an application of these principles to the present stage of the cultivation of poetry, and a defence of the attempt to idealize the modern forms of manners and opinions.
>
> (*Ibid.*, p. 158.)

The task of the poets is to realize this Idea of Good; they are 'the hierophants of an unapprehended inspiration; the mirrors of the gigantic shadows which futurity casts upon the present' (*Ibid.*, p. 159). This second part of his *Defence* was never written, but even in the first part Shelley assigns a revolutionary role to the poet. His own poetry, of course, associates the poet with the struggle for freedom;

> Most wretched men
> Are cradled into poetry by wrong,
> They learn in suffering what they reach in song.
> (*Julian and Maddalo.*)

Supreme amongst such rebels is his own Prometheus, a hierophantic figure who rescues men from tyranny and raises them to become the new gods.

More influential than either Keats or Shelley in establishing the general climate of thought after Coleridge was John Stuart Mill, who stood in the same relationship to the nineteenth as Locke to the eighteenth century. Mill knew and admired Coleridge's philosophy but, in spite of this, his account of the poetic imagination is fundamentally associative. With eighteenth-century writers like Alexander Gerard, and perhaps with Wordsworth's Preface to *Lyrical Ballads* in mind, he describes the imagination as an association of ideas or images governed by the feelings. Poets, he writes in *The Two Kinds of Poetry* (1833), are

> Those who are so constituted, that emotions are the links of association by which their ideas, both sensuous and spiritual, are connected together.
>
> (*Mill's Essays on Literature and Society*, ed. J. B. Schneewind, p. 119.)

In the same year, in the essay *What is Poetry?*, he declares:

> The object of poetry is confessedly to act upon the emotions; and therein is poetry sufficiently distinguished from what Wordsworth

affirms to be its logical opposite, namely, not prose, but matter of fact or science. The one addresses itself to the belief, the other to the feelings.

(*Ibid.*, pp. 103–4.)

However great and sincere his admiration for Coleridge, Mill's attitude to literature came to rest upon a sharp division between the logical and discursive powers of the mind on the one side, and the life of the emotions on the other. The unity upon which Coleridge had insisted, in which 'the whole soul of man' is engaged in poetic creation, is broken down and poetry for Mill becomes the organization of experience into an artistic pattern which will evoke a unity of emotional response; the value of poetry consists in its therapeutic effectiveness.

This is a view which, in our own day, I. A. Richards has advanced as being Coleridge's. Richards carried Victorian thought about poetry to its logical conclusion; he attempted to turn literary criticism into a science of the emotions and to assess literary value by a measurement of the emotional satisfaction it yielded. In this he was the heir both of Mill, who believed that truth was the province of science, and of Matthew Arnold, who believed that poetry would provide a religion without dogma as the faith of the future; that the poet would take the place of the priest 'to interpret human life afresh and to supply a new spiritual basis to it'. This is clearly seen in Richards's *Science and Poetry* (1926) where he refers to the collapse of our traditional beliefs and says:

We shall then be thrown back, as Matthew Arnold foresaw, upon poetry. It is capable of saving us; it is a perfectly possible means of overcoming chaos.

(pp. 82–3.)

But it is evident that the 'truth' of this poetic faith is little more than emotional reassurance. 'It will be admitted', he writes, in the chapter entitled 'Poetry and Beliefs',

– by those who distinguish between scientific statement, where truth is ultimately a matter of verification as this is understood in the laboratory, and emotive utterance, where 'truth' is primarily acceptability *by* some attitude, and more remotely is the acceptability *of* this attitude itself – that it is *not* the poet's business to make true statements.

Richards, while trying to confer the status of a science upon criticism, left poetry without any foundations other than the feelings. The relation he made between religion and poetry on the one side, and science and criticism on the other, was not the synthesis Coleridge had laboured to achieve. It is, indeed, as D. G. James's *Scepticism and Poetry* convincingly showed, more like a modern version of the behaviourist psychology advanced by Hartley, which Coleridge experienced as a dark night of the soul and which his theory of the imagination challenged in the most radical way.

Bibliography

List of Works Cited in the Text in Chronological Order. The place of publication is London unless otherwise stated.

PLATO, *Ion* (*The Dialogues of Plato*, trans. B. Jowett, 5 vols., Oxford, 1871).

SIDNEY, P., *An Apologie for Poetrie*, 1595, ed. G. Shepherd, 1964.

BACON, F., *The Advancement of Learning*, 1605 (*Critical Essays of the Seventeenth Century*, ed. J. E. Spingarn, Oxford, 1908).

MILTON, J., *The Reason of Church Government*, 1641 (*Critical Essays of the Seventeenth Century*, ed. J. E. Spingarn, Oxford, 1908).

Paradise Lost, 1667, ed. Helen Darbishire, Oxford, 1931.

HOBBES, T., *Answer to D'Avenant*, 1650 (*Critical Essays of the Seventeenth Century*, ed. J. E. Spingarn, Oxford, 1908).

Leviathan, 1651, ed. Michael Oakeshott, Oxford, 1946.

CUDWORTH, R., *True Intellectual System*, 1678.

DRYDEN, J., *Essays*, ed. W. P. Ker, Oxford, 1900.

LOCKE, J., *An Essay Concerning Human Understanding*, 1690, ed. A. C. Fraser, Oxford, 1894.

SHAFTESBURY, Third Earl of, *Characteristics*, 1711, ed. J. M. Robertson, 1900.

Several Letters, written to a Young Man at the University, 1716.

Second Characters, or the Language of Forms, ed. B. Rand, Cambridge, 1914.

ADDISON, J., *Spectator* papers *On the Pleasures of the Imagination*, 1712.

HUME, D., *A Treatise of Human Nature*, 1739, ed. A. D. Lindsay, 1911.

AKENSIDE, M., *The Pleasures of the Imagination*, 1744.
Odes on Several Subjects, 1745.

HARTLEY, D., *Observations on Man*, 1749.

BURKE, E., *A Philosophical Enquiry into the Sublime and Beautiful* (with an *Introd. On Taste*), 1757, ed. J. T. Boulton, 1958.

GERARD, A., *Essay on Genius*, 1774.

BLAKE, W., *There is No Natural Religion*, 1788.
All Religions are One, 1788.
The Everlasting Gospel, 1818.

KANT, I., *Critique of Aesthetic Judgment*, 1790, trans. J. C. Meredith, Oxford, 1911.

COLERIDGE, S. T., *The Statesman's Manual*, 1816.
Biographia Literaria, 1817, ed. J. Shawcross, Oxford, 1907.
Specimens of the Table Talk of the late S. T. Coleridge, ed. H. N. Coleridge, 1835.
Letters of S. T. Coleridge, ed. E. H. Coleridge, 2 vols., 1895.
The Complete Poetical Works, ed. E. H. Coleridge, Oxford, 1912.
Coleridge's Shakespearean Criticism, ed. T. M. Raysor, 1930, rev. 1960 (Everyman's Library).
Coleridge's Miscellaneous Criticism, ed. T. M. Raysor, 1936.
Collected Letters of S. T. Coleridge, ed. E. L. Griggs, 4 vols., Oxford 1956–9.
The Notebooks of S. T. Coleridge, ed. Kathleen Coburn, 1957–61.

KEATS, J., *Letters*, ed. M. B. Forman, 2 vols., 1931, final rev. 1952.

MILL, J. S., *The Two Kinds of Poetry* and *What is Poetry?* Both essays were published in the *Monthly Repository*, one in Jan., the other in Nov., 1833. (*Mill's Essays on Literature and Society*, ed. J. B. Schneewind, 1965.)

SHELLEY, P. B., *A Defence of Poetry*, 1840 (*Shelley's Literary and Philosophical Criticism*, ed. J. Shawcross, 1909).

RICHARDS, I. A., *Science and Poetry*, 1926.

A LIST OF CRITICAL WORKS

Books

ABRAMS, M., *The Mirror and the Lamp: Romantic Theory and the Critical Tradition*, New York, 1953.
A masterly survey of Romantic literary theory.

APPLEYARD, J. A., *Coleridge's Philosophy of Literature*, Oxford, 1966.
A most able study which relates Coleridge's theory of literature to his philosophical and religious interests.

BATE, W. J., *From Classic to Romantic: Premises of Taste in Eighteenth Century England*, Cambridge, Mass., 1946.

BRETT, R. L., *The Third Earl of Shaftesbury: A Study in Eighteenth Century Literary Theory*, 1951.
Contains a chapter which relates eighteenth-century theories of the imagination to Coleridge.
Reason and Imagination, 1960.
The first chapter reformulates Coleridge's theory in modern terms and another chapter interprets *The Ancient Mariner* in accordance with Coleridge's theory of the imagination.

FOGLE, R. H., *The Idea of Coleridge's Criticism*, 1962.
An excellent study of Coleridge as a critic.

HAYTER, A., *Opium and the Romantic Imagination*, 1968.
A fascinating account of drug addiction and the Romantic poets.

HOUSE, H., *Coleridge: The Clark Lectures 1951–52*, 1953.
A most perceptive study of Coleridge's poetry and literary theory.

JAMES, D. G., *Scepticism and Poetry: An Essay on the Poetic Imagination*, 1937.
A brilliant commentary which regards Coleridge's theory of the imagination as Kantian and is critical of I. A. Richards.
The Romantic Comedy, 1948.
Traces the decline of the Romantic conception of imagination in nineteenth-century poetry and criticism.

MUIRHEAD, J. H., *Coleridge as Philosopher*, 1930.
Somewhat out of date in view of recent scholarship, but still a standard work.

READ, H., *Coleridge as Critic*, 1949.
A good short account of Coleridge as a philosophical critic.

RICHARDS, I. A., *Coleridge on Imagination*, 1934.
Attempts to accommodate Coleridge's theory to Richards's own doctrines.

WILLEY, B., *Nineteenth Century Studies: Coleridge to Matthew Arnold*, 1949.
Contains an excellent first chapter on Coleridge; the remaining chapters are an indispensable guide to Victorian thought.

Essays and Articles

BATE, W. J. and BULLIT, J., 'Distinctions between Fancy and Imagination in Eighteenth Century Criticism', *Mod. Lang. Notes*, Jan., 1935.

BRETT, R. L., 'Coleridge's Theory of the Imagination', *Essays and Studies by Members of the English Association*, 1949.

COHEN, R., 'Association of Ideas and Poetic Unity', *Philological Quarterly*, 36 (1957).

HARDY, B., 'Distinction without Difference: Coleridge's Fancy and Imagination', *Essays in Criticism*, Oct., 1951.

KALLICK, M., 'The Association of Ideas and Critical Theory: Hobbes, Locke, and Addison', *English Literary History*, 12 (1945).

RAYSOR, T. M., 'Coleridge's Criticism of Wordsworth', *P.M.L.A.* June, 1939.

Index